EXCHANGE

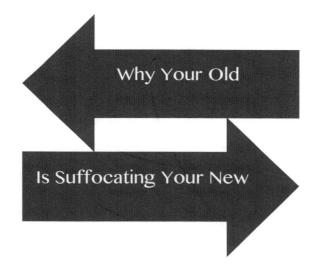

Why Your Old

Is Suffocating Your New

LAUREN A. WARD

KEEN
VISION
PUBLISHING

KNOXVILLE

Cover design by JP Designs Art
Author photograph by Project Rewired

Printed in the United States of America

ISBN-13: 978-0692752654

Keen Vision Publishing, LLC

www.keen-vision.com

ACKNOWLEDGEMENTS

I honor the following with my deepest gratitude:

Jesus Christ, my Lord, and Savior.

Mom and Dad, I've always thought about how I could repay you for all of your sacrifice, wisdom, love, and care. Then I figured, there would be nothing better than for you to witness me live a life pleasing to God and accomplish what He created me to do. Thank you for reminding me that it's fine to glean from others but to "get to know God for myself". Your words of wisdom and love resound in my heart always. I love you dearly.

Phillip and Kristen, thank you. You both are such a blessing and probably two of the most supportive people in my life! In different ways, you both helped make this particular project a success, and I can't thank you enough. Phil, It was during the time that you opened your space to me in grad school that this book was conceived. Thank you for always wanting to support however you can. Your heart is big and so giving, thank you.

Kristen, many of our conversations and experiences sparked ideas for what I share inside this book. Thank you for being a sounding board, for keeping the good talks (and even laughs!) rolling and being there through every step of the journey that I share inside! I can't wait to see more of what the two of you will accomplish through your personal journeys. Love always.

Melissa E., Crystal P., Nykia W., Takeya W., & Brittany M., You each played an important role during the transitional time that the idea for this book was birthed. Your friendship is beyond appreciated. Love you.

To Ms. Linda, thank you for your prayers and love.

To my current pastors, Pastor Kerrick and Raquel Bulter, and previous pastors, Anthony and SaBrina Wheeler thank you for your shepherding, your leadership and for being a constant blessing to me. Love you all.

To my prayer group: Thank you for taking out the time to believe God with me for Kingdom success. Our prayers have moved Heaven, and this is just the beginning!

To you, the reader, may you take this and run with it. Sometimes slower, sometimes faster but never stopping. There's a race you must finish. Let this book spark a desire for you to pick up a much greater book, the Bible. I'm rooting for you! God bless.

My sincerest prayer is that every person who touches this book comes to know Jesus Christ as their personal Lord and Savior.

ABOUT THE AUTHOR

Lauren A. Ward is an *influencer* and *innovative* thinker who has made an impact on many lives through various mediums. She is a Birmingham, Alabama native and a current resident of Atlanta, Georgia. Lauren holds a Bachelor's of Arts and Sciences from The University of Alabama (Tuscaloosa, Alabama) and Master's of Science from Alabama A&M University (Huntsville, Alabama). She is a speech Language Pathologist by profession, and a servant of the Kingdom by lifestyle. Lauren has a heart for mentorship, leadership and teaching the word of God. She shares a compassion for people who desire "more" out of life. Lauren is passionate about pushing them towards achieving that "more" through Christ and understanding their purpose. She is the visionary and founder of The Loft, an innovative Christian organization that has encouraged the hearts of many to "Live Life Forward". Lauren is also privileged in serving as a leader of the national young Christian women's ministry, Saved in the City. Now, launching her first book, Exchange, Lauren hopes to encourage many to make the mental, habitual, spiritual and practical adjustments to make the changes they were created to make.

CONTENTS

INTRODUCTION

From time to time, people inquire about how I've been able to achieve so much at such a young age. Without a doubt, I know my success is only a result of God's unconditional love. In a short amount of time, God has done exceptional things in my life, and I am grateful. Honestly, I haven't always been at this place, and I still have far to go.

One day, I stood in the mirror preparing for work and heard, *"Will you make change?"* Naturally, I thought to myself, *"Will I make change? Change for what, exactly?"*

Immediately, I assumed God was speaking to me about a money matter, but His question didn't make much sense or *cents*. At the time, I didn't have any "serious" money. I also did not have an answer for His strange question. I dismissed the thought (as I had done many times before) but that didn't make the thought go away. We all know how persistent God can be! This question echoed in my mind for weeks. Then it dawned on me. God's question wasn't a question for me to answer. It was a statement for me to understand. God was speaking to my heart – not my wallet. When God places a question on our hearts, He isn't looking for our perfect reply; He's looking for our attention. I love how God grabs our attention to teach us principles we never knew we needed to know. Clarity doesn't always come easily. We must seek (search relentlessly & hunt) to understand how He desires to improve the condition of our hearts.

God began to show me that He has something special for each of us. Not just anything, but His personal plans and purpose for our lives – what He created us to do. In addition to having something for us, He wants something from us. God desires that we release our tight grip on the dead-end plans we unknowingly have for ourselves. He wants us to exchange our chaotic desires for His perfect plan.

"I must decrease that you may increase." (John 3:30)

God stopped me in the tracks of my life and began to redirect me. For the first time, I could see what I had never seen before. I had been living life through the lens of what I saw for myself. My view of my life had gotten me nowhere fast. I realized that my plans for my life were just as tiny as the bathroom in which I stood when God spoke. God had already mapped out a huge destiny for me. He didn't need my help nor my plans. He only needed my heart.

I thought about the current condition of my life. I didn't have much of anything. Everything I had invested in was slowly falling apart or already in pieces. I had an appetite for what the world offered me and chased it until I was empty. I mistakenly thought that knowing of God, and being raised in a church was enough. I couldn't have been more wrong. I was sure of one thing, and one thing only. It was time for me to dig deeper into my relationship with God and get direction on what He had created me to do.

Now, let's talk about you. *What are you doing here?* Don't give me that look. You were put on this Earth to do something. If what you were created to do could easily be done by someone else, God wouldn't need you, and *you wouldn't be here.* You have a God-given purpose created just for you. We've all been assigned to do something great, but many of us never tap into a fraction of what God has placed within us because we never master **the art of exchange**.

So, what's the art of exchange, you ask? The concept is actually quite simple. Remember those clothes you hurriedly bought without trying on? If it was something you loved, I'm sure you simply went back to the same store, and exchanged it for the size you needed, right? That, my friend, was an exchange. Just as we sometimes select the wrong sizes, we also select the *wrong habits.*

Unlike exchanging clothes, we take entirely too long to exchange habits we don't need.

It's a tough pill to swallow, but know that you are not alone. Personally, I had been wearing things that didn't fit my destiny for an over-extended period of time. For the life of me, I couldn't figure out why I wasn't moving forward. I desired more, but my habits were not capable of producing more. I added more responsibilities and accepted different opportunities, but because I never exchanged my way of doing things I remained stagnant in my purpose. My life did not advance until I realized that attempting to change required me to exchange my old habits, mindsets, and perspectives for new habits, mindsets, and perspectives that fit my destiny.

In order to live the abundant life God planned for us, we must release our poor lifestyle practices. We can't allow old habits to linger. The art of exchange requires us to be brutally honest about our weaknesses. Whatever we don't get rid of, *we leave as an option*. The truth of the matter is, new isn't new if old is mixed in. What we are willing to exchange determines how well we will be positioned for God's best. Exchange is the beginning of expectation and expectation is the beginning of faith! In this book, you'll learn that exchange is the necessary preparation for any promise. I will share my personal journey as a catalyst to motivate you to look and live forward!

Prepare to be challenged to implement Godly principles, wise practices, and practical habits. Let's be honest, taking a passive approach and living on the shallow end of fulfillment is disappointing. Don't be afraid to stretch! It's time you made operating in excellence a lifestyle.

Before you begin this book, I have been instructed to tell you that God wants to open your eyes to things you've never seen before. He wants to reveal the truths and insights you are blind to. Isn't it strange that our eyes can be open-wide shut? We have to want them to be open. So, before you read another word, say this quick, yet powerful prayer. *"God, please open the eyes of my heart and flood them with Your light. At this moment, I exchange my limited sight for Yours. Amen."*

You don't need an explanation, an excellent history or exemplary credentials to practice the art of exchange. You were qualified at the cross never to get stuck with another bad deal again. *Cha-ching!* Let's exchange!

CHAPTER ONE
THE BEST BOSS EVER

For reasons I cannot explain, many people naturally do not embrace change, *myself included.* Most tend to actually resist change, desperately seek stability, and would prefer to not have their 'boat rocked'. We crave equilibrium and find it easier to simply leave things alone even when we know they do not work. *At all.* We are bold enough to bare the pain of a harmful relationship, a failing business, and other strained situations because we are not courageous enough to allow something to change! As much as we fight against it, we should keep in mind that change is actually essential for growth. A seed cannot remain a seed if we want to see a flower; therefore, at some point a change must occur for true growth to take place!

Unfortunately, what we've always seen easily becomes our norm. And how we function may be, in fact, more dysfunctional than we're willing to admit. It is unexplainably easy to become our past experiences, but what we've seen should not automatically become what we do. We were not created to mimic madness nor to find complacency in chaos, but rather to create change when necessary. We were created by the God to do just what He did, *create!* However, change cannot be created by repetition but rather replacement.

"Before I shaped you in the womb, I knew all about you. Before you saw the light of day, I had holy plans for you." *(Jeremiah 1:5 MSG)*

What Qualifies You for the Job

God intentionally designed each of us for our earthly jobs. God began with a purpose, then created us to fit the purpose. Our purposes were not created for us! We were created for our purposes. For this reason, it is important for us to have a clear understanding of what God has created us to do. Without our purposes, we would be useless.

Does the thought of having a God-given purpose frighten you? If so, it's probably because you feel unequipped. Fear not. During our creation, God equipped us with the necessary tools to do what we were created to do. Everything you need to carry out your assignments here on Earth was included in your DNA.

When we work outside of our purpose, we find ourselves stretched thin, extremely tired, or unmotivated. We feel this way because we are attempting to do things we were not equipped to do. God would not call you to a bowl of soup and hand you a knife! He gives exactly what we need to properly and successfully achieve our ordained assignments!

For everything God desires to do on earth, He needs a body to do it through. Your creation qualified you for your calling. If you have a body, you can be used by God! We're pretty great, but we haven't done anything great enough to qualify ourselves. God has. Our response to God's call is simply making ourselves available to Him. Our availability is an invitation for God to do exceedingly abundantly above what we could ever imagine! (Ephesians 3:20)

God Employs our Past

The thought of moving towards a bright future is often hindered by the lingering shadows of our past. Memories of past experiences remind us of who we *once were*. These memories attempt to reel us back into our old ways of doing things. It never fails. Our past will always try to work against us, but if we give our pasts to God, He will make them work for us! He employs our history and causes every situation, *good or bad,* to be used for our good. The world uses our past to determine whether or not we qualify for our future, but God prequalifies us and does not hold our past against us. Every broken situation can become a stepping-stone to destiny when we give our past over to God.

Being Found Doing Nothing

As strange as it sounds, doing something that doesn't matter can be just as invaluable as doing nothing at all. In the Bible, Jesus tells many interesting stories. In several of those stories, He often uses the parallel of an employer and his workers as a way of describing the Kingdom of God. In one of His stories, (the Parable of the vineyard workers in Matthew 20), Jesus tells about an owner who goes out early in the morning to hire men to work in his vineyard. In these times, those who wanted a job would come to the market place with their tools in hand and wait for future employers. Employers would visit the marketplace and hire men who were already equipped for the jobs they needed to be done. The employers would extend an invite to the workers, and the workers would decide if they wanted to work with the employer.

"For the Kingdom of God is like a landowner who went out early in the morning to hire men to work in his vineyard. He agreed to pay them a denarius for the day and sent them into his vineyard. About the third hour, he went out and saw others standing in the marketplace doing nothing. He told them, you also go work in my vineyard." (Matthew 20:1-7)

All those who were hired by the vineyard owner were found "doing nothing". Wait, they were doing *nothing?* So, let's get this straight. These workers stood in the middle of a marketplace, waited, and did nothing. In the middle of all the buying and trading, huge deal making, opportunities of networking and free marketing, these workers waited and did nothing? To many of us, this sounds absurd. After all, they had everything they needed to be successful. The marketplace was the perfect opportunity for them to do other things as they waited to be employed, but these men were found doing nothing. In this parable, Jesus is attempting to teach us a very important principle.

Until we allow God into our lives, everything we do can

be comparable to doing nothing. Until we live for God, we haven't truly begun to live at all. We must constantly seek the difference between what He is calling us to do and random opportunities. Doing something "random" is "doing nothing". When we take on random opportunities, we still have that nagging itch or desire for "more" despite all the good things happening in our lives. This is why so many people can have a great job, a great spouse, good grades, a beautiful home, more degrees and money than one could imagine yet still feel *unfulfilled*. Good never feels good enough without God.

You Are Worth the Risk

I don't know many bosses who would hire an at-risk person. Think about it, would you hire an emotional, inconsistent worker with a sketchy background and a resume of doing nothing? You probably wouldn't. Only God would employ a wretch like that. He actually desires to use those type of people. God thinks we are worth the risk! He is able to look past where we are because He sees where He is taking us. Despite the mistakes we make, He sees the value He placed in us before our conception.

Worth: The level at which someone or something

deserves to be valued.

Every creation has a creator. The creator gives worth to what He created. Before anyone had an opinion, God undoubtedly designed and defined us. He placed a value on us that is neither adjustable or negotiable. For example, a diamond found in a puddle of mud is just as valuable as a diamond found in a case at the finest jewelry store. Where we are in life does not change who we are destined to be. People's recognition of our value doesn't change the value God has already placed on us. *Let's be honest.* We've been overlooked quite a few times. We've been mistreated more times than we care to mention. This is why it is important for us to know who we are in God. The best way to remain confident of who we are is by studying what God has said about us. These truths, found in His word, replace the poor images painted in our minds by our pasts and other people. When we fail to renew our minds through His word, we give people and situations the power to make us think our worth has diminished.

Just as we get up every morning and wash our faces, we should wash ourselves in God's word. Cleansing our minds with the Word of God removes filthy thought patterns and leaves our thoughts full of faith and power.

After reading the word, take what you've read and make a confession of it. To confess is to declare. Make your confession personal by inserting your name in the scripture that applies to your life because it is, in fact, for you! Whatever you hear more, you will believe more. Faith comes by hearing. Keep saying the word, keep hearing the word, and you will no longer be plagued by an innate tendency to allow your past and others to define your value. We are an extension of The One who created us. Don't just stand there doing nothing. There is still much work to be done, and God is still hiring. *Will you work in the Kingdom?*

CHAPTER TWO
BAD SPILLS

Nothing new will happen if we do what we have always have done. Remember, exchange means we must replace the old with the new.

"Remove the old wineskin. Neither is new wine put into old wineskins. If it is, the skins burst and the wine is spilled, and the skins are destroyed. But new wine is put into fresh wineskins, and so both are preserved." (Matthew 9:17)

In this verse, we are encouraged to remove the *old* and replace it with the *new*. This scripture shows us that it is impossible to hold new material in old containers without the material or the container being ruined. In the same light, we cannot experience the newness of life with old mindsets, habits, or heart conditions. We have to replace where we hold our thoughts, desires, and dreams. A contaminated heart will produce contaminated desires, attitudes, and actions which produce contaminated lives. Just as a corrupt mind will produce corrupt thoughts, decisions, and perspectives on life.

Imagine pouring fresh water into a filthy, molded, cracked jar. The water will unquestionably become dirty and slowly leak through the cracks. Nothing about the fresh water will change the condition of that jar. Often, instead of replacing the container, we keep trying to fill it only to become empty again. We get away with this habit because the containers of our hearts and minds aren't visible on the outside. People assume we are well put together even though we are empty on the inside. Are you ready for the good news? We don't have to stay this way. It is God's pleasure to exchange our broken, corrupt, and contaminated containers for new ones. His word promises to give us beauty for ashes and restoration for our souls.

Pull from the Root

Jesus replied, "Every plant not planted by my heavenly Father will be uprooted." (Matthew 15:13)

So, how do we begin this exchange? The first level of exchange *is getting rid of the root.* The root of a thing determines its origin. As long as the root is present, only what it produces can grow in that particular space. Many of us find ourselves only attacking what surfaces. As a result, we keep slipping in the same old spill. Our cycles of failure are a direct result of not getting to the root of the problem.

We find ourselves leaving relationship after relationship, job after job, and church after church for the same reason. At some point, we have to realize that if we continue to encounter the same issue in every situation, the problem may not be the situation. The problem may very well be ourselves and our approach. If we can manage to dig deep and identify the root, we can undoubtedly begin to see a shift in our situations. This change can only happen when we:

REALIZE Identify the root of the problem and the source of the cycle. This calls for us to live in the reality of what takes place. It takes a mature person to look inwardly for the cause of constant conflict.

RID Some trash never makes it to the waste basket because we refuse to identify the trash for what it is-- trash. We find ourselves hoarding onto useless things with hope that they will someday become useful. After you identify the root, it's time to extract it and any other weeds that have grown. We must completely destroy the root and prepare the grounds of hearts for what will be planted in its place. This is a crucial step of exchange that is often avoided. Adding new seeds to existing weeds is not grounds for new growth. Whatever we refuse to uproot will, in time, grow again. This step is also most resisted because it's hard to let go of the messy, yet comfortable circumstances we've grown accustomed to. During this step, it is important to keep in mind your desired level of excellence. Don't allow where you are to keep you from where you are going!

RUN After removing ourselves from fruitless thoughts, actions, and habits, we must run in the opposite direction. Our focus is now on living the life God called us to live. As tempting as it may seem, we can not hang around and flirt with what once was. Satan will always use its familiarity to us to try to lure us back in. This is why it is so imperative that we don't allow ourselves to get comfortable in comfort. Once you are on track for what God is calling you to, run your race, and don't look back. After a while, the impact of the past will wear off, and your ability to resist the comfort of the past will become stronger.

"Unless the Lord builds the house, those who build it labor in vain." (Psalms 127:1)

Everything we do in our lives is the reality of what we live in. The houses we've built on bad ground don't stand for long. As a matter of fact, the MSG version says unless God doesn't build the house, the builders only build shacks. More than anything, a desire to please God has to be our focus. His desires should override our own. We have to want to Him and His plans to be our number one goal.

God is so intentional and loving. He doesn't allow things that are not purposeful to last, nor is He obligated to sustain what He did not initiate or ordain. Living our lives on any other foundation other than God is like building a home of popsicle sticks and expecting it to function as a well-built construction with top of the line amenities. It just won't happen!

We often pray for things that we haven't been prepared for and become upset when we don't receive what we asked for in prayer. At a time in my life when I was believing God for some pretty incredible things, I didn't understand why in the world I had not seen the answer I sought Him about. I felt like I was being stripped. God dealt with my heart and exposed some of the holes in my love walk with others. I couldn't believe it. I was beyond frustrated. I thought God had forgotten about me and allowed me to experience discomfort. One day, God spoke to my heart and revealed that He refused to allow my life to be built on such a rocky foundation. Everything I asked for required a foundation of love, faith, obedience, and wisdom. God kept me from building on a foundation He knew would not sustain the structure of my purpose and His huge plan for my life. I was officially under construction. All of the cracks, breaks, and weak parts of my foundation needed to be fixed. There was only one builder who could properly do the job.

The strength of a structure is entirely dependent upon its foundation. A weak foundation precedes a poorly developed building. Don't fret if some areas of your life require some rebuilding from God. It isn't a waste of time, but rather time well spent! Building on our own is labor that is simply not worth it. Building on our own is tiring, hard, and vain. The sooner we allow the reconstruction to begin, the sooner we can begin to experience the unimaginable and incredible works of God.

CHAPTER THREE

PUT YOUR FOOT DOWN!

"Be strong and courageous, for you are the one who will lead these people to possess all the land I swore to their ancestors I would give them. Be strong and very courageous."

These were the words God spoke to Joshua after giving Joshua his assignment. Joshua's God-given assignment revealed that he was chosen to do something in a *particular* place that would affect a *particular* group of people. Let's take a closer look:

Joshua will lead *(the what)* **these people** *(the who),* **to possess the land God swore to their ancestors** *(the where)* **and it will cause them to prosper in the promises of God** *(the why).*

Now, what about you? Do you know *the what, who, where and why* of your purpose? God has assigned us to certain places and people for a certain result. This verse proves just that. Understanding these aspects of our purpose launches us into a life of living forward. Living forward is a life of direction pursued by those who seek to fulfill their God-given purpose. Living forward forces one to constantly deny the four letter word – fear. It requires one to move boldly and fearlessly in the direction God has predestined for them.

In Joshua 1, God tells Joshua four times to "be strong and very courageous". From this repeated instruction, we can glean that one of the largest deterrents to exploring purpose is *fear*. Fear will always rear its ugly head once we have been presented with purpose. Knowing this in advance can help us decide to move forward in the presence of fear. Verse three says:

"Every place where the sole of your foot shall tread, that I have given to you." (Joshua 1:3)

Initially, we could think that everywhere we step is going to be ours. But there is a deeper revelation here. The verse mentions that everywhere the *sole of our foot treads*, will be ours. The sole of your foot anatomically refers to the bottom of your foot, including the heel. Anytime the bottom of a person's foot touches the ground; they are no longer considered to be 'tip-toeing.' Walking on the tip of your toes is expected when a person is sneaking around, hiding, or unsure of what's ahead. On the contrary, a person whose sole hits the ground is making sure, confident, and bold steps! Bold faith is not sneaky and unsure. It does not pause at corners to decide if it will proceed or not. It does not wait for the approval of others and does not care about having to make a little noise.

The message here is that we don't walk by what we see we walk by faith with confidence. We don't tiptoe around because we "aren't sure exactly of how things will turn out". We trust God to do what He's always done -- meet and exceed every need we have!

So often, our steps are much less than a true step of faith. Instead of walking boldly in faith, we tip-toe around what we believe God is calling us to. We tiptoe because we assume that we have to know everything about the ground we are stepping into. The strength of our faith walk is not dependent on our trust in the ground, but our trust in God.

Fear reminds us that we have no idea about the next step. It reminds us of every "What if" possible. It keeps the soles of our feet off the ground. We must exchange how we *respond to fear* so that we do not allow it to *affect our walk.*

Remember this, the enemy will try to use the very thing God called you to do to scare you. The enemy's plan is to deceive us into believing what we see. He tricks us into acting on the images of failure he paints for us. He works tirelessly to rob us of our trust in God. When we are unaware of his schemes, we slowly lose our certainty about what God has spoken and instructed. The enemy does not want us strong and courageous. An ingredient of courage is confidence, and faith is the confidence that we have in God. We have to literally and physically put our foot down. Faith is an action word and requires us to move on what we say we believe. We move on the promises of God knowing that we cannot fail because God nor His word ever fails. He covers us on every side. God goes before us and sends favor ahead of us. He's with us as strength & wisdom on the right and left. He even comes behind us to help us recover from things that have happened in our past. Who could be afraid to walk in purpose with a God like that?

CHAPTER FOUR

WHAT DO YOU SEE?

t's hard to move with no clue about the next step. Trust me; I've gotten lost more times than I can count! When I first got my driver's license, I probably used more gas aimlessly driving around lost than I did getting where I needed to go.

A good set of directions is great for driving. (I should know!) Directions provide step by step turns, the total number of miles left until the destination is reached, and even an estimated time of arrival. Super convenient, right? Nevertheless, our familiarity with an instantaneous list of directions gives us an unrealistic expectation of how we navigate in our spiritual lives. A part of us would love the convenient turn-by-turn guide (with the familiar monotone navigation voice blaring "Turn left in 400 feet") and start-to-finish steps as we move on our spiritual journey. But God doesn't lead us in that way. God gives more *direction* rather than *directions.* We will never see all of the steps at once for a God-sized plan. There's simply no way we could handle all that God desires to do in our lives at one time. If we did, we'd also have a very plain God, who operates on the same level of thinking as we do. He wouldn't be very miraculous or magnificent at all – He'd be just like us! God is not confined to two lefts and a right. His ways and thoughts are higher than ours. Doing things our way can not take us to where God is trying to take us! He's much more complex than just one destination. He puts us on a journey and guides us, yet does not force us. He gives us instruction and desires us to move in faith. Once we make the instructed move, He gives us the next one.

Paint a Picture

Imagination is not just for kids. Imagining is creating an image in your mind about what God has placed on your heart. All of our good thoughts, daydreaming and imagining are the beginning steps of faith. The pictures we are able to paint for ourselves can be pretty powerful! If you can see in your heart what you can't see in your hand, what's in your heart will sooner or later be in your hand.

"As a man thinketh in His heart, so is he." (Proverbs 23:7)

What we set our attention and thoughts on will eventually surface in our lives. For this reason, we must do as God told Joshua to do in Joshua 1:8, meditate on the law day and night. Faith cannot be something we just talk about or claim to possess. Faith has to become our reality! Many of us face difficulty believing the promises of God because they have yet to become real to us! Because of our unbelief, imagination and meditation are so important. We can't just read the word; we must also meditate on it. Meditating on the word makes the promises of God our reality. Meditation brings revelation! So how do we meditate on the word? When we read it, we must say it over and over in our hearts and minds until it sinks into us and becomes our expectations. Through meditation, we receive revelation. A revelation of the word is like a form of transportation. It gives direction and takes us somewhere we couldn't go without it.

Vision Gives Life

Most of us have learned the hard way that moving with no vision may not be moving forward at all. The funny thing about movement is that movement is in fact motion, but motion does not guarantee that we are headed anywhere. If you've ever ran on a treadmill, then you know that it is very possible to go nowhere fast. Running on a treadmill is exactly what moving without vision looks like. Moving with vision, however, is always a key step to any great accomplishment. Vision is one way God shows us what He sees for us. When we allow ourselves to see what He sees, what we see around us no longer matters.

"Where there is no vision, the people perish." (Proverbs 29:18)

Vision is divine guidance and without it, we yield or give into the world's way of doing things. In other words, without vision, we begin to die spiritually. Another version of this verse says, 'If people can't see what God is doing, they stumble all over themselves; but when they attend to what He reveals, they are most blessed." God is always revealing things to us, but are we paying attention to what He shows us? Are we more concerned with what we see that we don't allow ourselves to see what God sees for us?

Receive Vision

One intense experience that comes along with vision is the burden of the cause and the people. Like any other burden, it's a heavy load. In this case, however, the burden is not physical but spiritual. Burdens create an intense passion and a powerful drive that gives us the strength to do what would otherwise wear us out.

"And I will stand my watch and set myself on the rampart, And watch to see what He will say to me, And what I will answer when I am corrected. Then the Lord answered me and said. "Write the vision and make it plain on tablets, That he may run who reads it. For the vision is yet for an appointed time; But at the end it will speak and it will not lie. Though it tarries, wait for it." (Habakkuk 2:1-5)

In this scripture, the prophet Habakkuk stood on a watchtower to wait for vision from God. We see where he went to hear and receive from God, but we often overlook what took him to his watchtower in the first place. Burden! Habakkuk was extremely upset and passionately burdened about the state of the people near him. He went to God in tears and cried out about what he saw. His burden of the strife and violence among his people gave him the endurance to stand and wait for vision. If it almost brings you to tears and simultaneously gives you energy, then it probably is a portion of your personal passion. Passion is a hint to purpose.

Publish Your Vision

I once heard someone say, *"What's spoken is soon forgotten, but what's written is more lasting."* Despite how bad we may need something, it's hard to commit it to memory. We can indeed need several items from the grocery store and still not remember to grab them once we get there. There's something about seeing your thoughts on paper! It brings about a reality that you don't realize in casual conversation. Writing your thoughts gives them weight and makes them official. Seeing your vision on paper shows you exactly where you are. One night years ago, I had grown tired of ignoring God's nudges, so I sat and wrote down the vision He had shown me. I wrote everything that moved me, and also the things that frustrated me. I had never been so courageous to write on paper the vision that God wrote in my heart. It was refreshing to see what God had been saying to me. Even though the vision had not taken place, I was able to see it happening. When we receive a vision from God, He desires us to write it plainly, without our opinions, reservations or reluctant rationales. Writing it plainly means leaving it just as God give it to us.

In addition to writing the vision, we actually have to pick it back up. Keeping our vision in sight is just as important as writing it. The more we look at it, the more we expect it. No good vision remains a vision. At some point, visions must become a victory! When the vision remains in front of us, we confidently expect victory.

Not Everyone Sees What You See

When I first moved to Atlanta, Georgia, I couldn't fully unpack before God began to ask me more questions I could not answer. I began to receive the vision to impact a particular group of people in the city. As God downloaded the vision into me, I was blown away by what I saw. It was such a bizarre vision that I had to share it with someone. God had given me the vision of a Saturday night worship experience for believers. I'll never forget the responses I received after sharing my vision. They reminded me of my reality, and how unlikely it was to see the vision carried out. They combated the vision with the most doubtful questions ever. People ran off a laundry list of facts. Since what I saw in my heart did not yet exist, it was a struggle to make others understand what they could not see. Their responses didn't necessarily come from a negative place. They spoke according to their own faith. God did not give them the vision, so I couldn't expect them to have the faith to see it without seeing it. The truth of the matter is, everyone won't get it, and that's okay. Everyone doesn't possess the visual capabilities for your God-sized vision. Don't be discouraged by other's lack of vision for your vision. Instead, guard your God-given vision against those who don't quite understand the move of God. Faith has become your sight. Be patient with others. Their disbelief or lack of faith is only a testament to the level of faith they exercise in their own lives. Pray for them and refrain from sharing your visions with them.

Opened Gates and Closed Doors

Our eyes and ears are the gates to our souls and minds. They're considered gates because they guard what goes in, which in turn, determines our wills and emotions. What enters our souls and minds determines what we desire and how we feel. Our gates monitor how we are fed spiritually. When we allow ourselves to see and hear negativity, we feel negative, think negatively, and believe negativity.

"Faith comes by hearing." (Romans 10:17a)

What we hear can either build us in faith or boost the level of fear that exists in our lives. For this reason, we must be careful about what we see and hear. We can't allow just anything to come in. What we let in, we eventually see come out. When a person desires to grow in purpose, they must become intentional. This is how we experience a level of purpose we have never experienced before. Intentionality requires us to be productive with our time. We must want both purposeful and productive days in which we get a lot done. We do this by guarding our gates. Observe what you let in on a daily basis. Think about what you allow yourself to hear and see. If you spend the majority of your day feeding your mind with negative TV shows and empty entertainment such as social media, then you probably aren't as productive. Set boundaries. Put a limit on time snatching activities that waste your time and leave you empty. Avoid listening to cheap talk i.e. gossiping, complaining and negativity. It's imperative that we keep the right desires, emotions, and thoughts. When I want to hear God on a specific situation, I turn off the things that cause the eyes and ears of my soul to be clogged. I listen to God throughout the day. I meditate on His thoughts and what He desires me to know. I listen for God's whisper as I work and think about what He shares. I change what I allow myself to think about. What we think about is essentially who we become. We think, then say, and finally, see it happen. The word tells us exactly what to think on:

"And now, dear brothers, whatever is true, whatever is honorable, and right, and pure, and lovely, and admirable. Think about things that are excellent and worthy of praise." (Philippians 4:8)

Here's the obvious: none of these things are negative! However, many of the thoughts that cross our minds daily are very negative in nature. Whether we know it or not, everyone has meditated before! Meditation is easy. During meditation, we continuously think of a thought, song, or something someone has said. During meditation, we think on these things until they speak to us and move us to feel a certain way. Think about the arguments, fights, or situations that took a turn for the worse due to your own response. It all started with meditation.

Just as we've meditated negatively, we can meditate positively. Instead of meditating on what people say, meditate on what God says. Switch out secular music for worship and motivational songs. We have the power replace bad thoughts with thoughts that are good, lovely and pure. The Bible is designed to speak to whatever we face in life. Find scriptures that speak to your situation and allow a beautiful picture of hope to be painted in your mind. To live in faith, we must believe and see in faith!

CHAPTER FIVE

KEEP THE MAIN THING, THE MAIN THING

I once heard of a family who left their home in the New York and moved to the country to open a ranch. Several months later, family and friends came to visit the family at their new home. They asked how the ranch was going, and the father replied, "Well, we had a bit of a setback. When the time came to choose the name of the ranch, I thought it should be named The Bar J. Well, Mother proposed the name The Suzy Q. My son thought The Flying W would be a much better name, and my daughter protested that it should be called The Lazy L. We could never agree on any one name, so we called the ranch The Bar J-Suzy Q-Flying W-Lazy Y Ranch. Unfortunately, none of the cattle survived the branding."

The main point of the ranch was to farm, raise cattle and have them bred. The name of the ranch was a small part of the ranch's purpose. Because they lost focus of the priority, they lost everything! All of their cattle died from branding. They all got what they wanted, but in the process, they lost the worth of their vision.

This is often a setback in many of our lives. We become so concerned with things that don't matter and miss out on the big picture! We must keep our minds focused on the bigger picture. There is no productivity in getting stuck on one part of the vision.

Even though something is important, that does not mean it is imperative for the moment. One of the biggest deterrents to progress is distractions. In the story above, the ranch was much more important than the name. Unfortunately, they didn't make the ranch their priority. What is a priority? A priority is something considered as more important than anything else. If everything on our list is important, we actually don't have any priorities at all! Priorities help us to balance and work productively. Priorities have hidden returns when placed in the correct place. You'll know when something in is the right place because of the results it produces.

The B Word

Busyness. We were all called to do something, but we weren't called to do everything. I used to be utterly convinced that the people who made the most impact in the world were the ones who were outrageously busy and didn't have a single second of time to do anything. Thankfully, that's not the truth! Juggling twenty things at once seems intriguing, but it is actually more of an act than an assignment. God does not desire us to be so overwhelmed that we never find time to include Him. Busyness is false progress! To be effective at anything, we can't do everything at once. A person doing everything is probably not sure of what they need to be doing. When someone is sure of what they need to be doing, they understand that they can't accept every opportunity or offer. We must apply rules to what we allow to enter our lives. A knock doesn't get you noticed, and every visit isn't valuable. Don't allow things into your life just because it came by! Opportunities are not assignments. We can filter the tasks we take on by asking three simple questions.

1. Does this bring God glory?
2. Is this an assignment or just another opportunity?
3. Is this a priority or a preference?

When we get rid of distractions, we can better see the things we need to give our time and attention. Distractions sometimes pose as priorities. Every so often, it is good to take inventory of everything on our plate, decipher what is important, and what is simply clutter. It's not only about having what we need to make change, but also getting rid of what we don't need. Start by looking at your last three days and account for each hour of the day. Compare the hours spent being productive and hours spent distracted. Pinpoint your distractions, and plan to replace them with productive tasks. A purposeful person is a good steward of time and refuses to spend their time on things that are not important.

CHAPTER SIX

GOOD GIFTS, STRANGE PACKAGES

Take a moment and think back over all of the many times you've received a gift in your life. Now and then, we receive gifts from people who love us. The best part of receiving a gift is the suspense of unwrapping it. Oh, the joy of tearing at the tightly taped sides of the box, ripping the paper into shreds, and bulldozing the box open to see your gift. Can you remember a time where you received a gift and decided that you didn't care to open it? Have you ever put a gift to the side and decided to open it later? Probably not. The suspense of an unwrapped present is too much for anyone to ignore.

What if we were as eager about uncovering our God-given spiritual gifts as we were about unwrapping gifts from people? What if we were confident in knowing that we are, in fact, flesh-wrapped gifts from God to the world? What if we were relentless in our search to learn how to use our gifts to change the world? We would be unstoppable! Unfortunately, we spend much of our lives looking everywhere for what's already inside of us. We are our own greatest resource. Let's face it-- it's extremely hard to use what you don't know you have. Sadly, too many people cannot begin to tell you what's inside of them. Ladies and gentlemen, we've got work to do!

One of the many names God uses to describe believers is vessels or containers filled with treasures. He creates, makes, molds, and shapes us into clay containers. He fills us with unique gifting, talents, and abilities. Just like all other treasures, everything He places in us is highly valuable. Our treasure is a part of why we are here on earth. God ensured that everything we need to be successful was stored in us. It is frustrating to suffocate the very thing you were created for. Decide now that you will awaken everything God has given you.

Start by thinking of yourself as a container. Ask God to show you what is inside of you, teach you how to use it for His glory, and send you daily reminders of who He has created you to be.

When I bought my Jeep earlier this year, it took over 30 minutes for the salesperson to give me a rundown of all of the functions and features that came with the car. As he spoke, I slipped in and out of paying attention. I kept thinking about things that had nothing to do with purchasing a car. After many minutes of drifting in and out of his sales spill, he finally wrapped up with, "And, I'm sure you'll love that feature".

"Wait, what feature, again?" I asked. I was completely lost. I actually had to ask him to give me a quick review. I knew there were secret compartments, different features, and amazing capabilities I would not have known if I didn't take the time to learn about my new truck now. The same goes for us. It is imperative that we explore the different things God has given us to propel us into our destiny! What's inside of you is a hint to your career, streams of income, and responsibility to others. Your God-given gift will profit you and the Kingdom of God. You must first take the time to listen to what God says about your gift. One day, we will all have to answer about how we used our gifts. *What will your answer be?*

Many of us only dig into one or two obvious gifts or talents. I believe there's much more to be pulled out. I was guilty of this as well. It wasn't until I began to explore the idea that maybe there's more inside of me that God began to reveal to me the many facets of my gifts. I will forever "fan the flame" of what He put in me.

Compare Yourself to Yourself

Why is it that we can see the gifts of others, but not ourselves? We compare our gifts with others and think less of who we are if we can't do the things they do. Comparing ourselves to others is a bad habit to have. We are not here to compete with others who have different gifts. We are here to connect with them to carry out the vision God has given us. Beware of competing with those you should be partnering with. The only person you need to compete with is the person you were yesterday. Compare yourself to yourself! By doing this, we ensure that we never become complacent in our current level of proficiency.

Connections are extremely important in the Kingdom of God. You don't need to know how to do everything. You only need God to connect you with the right people. So often, I would make a request of God and instead of giving me what I asked for, He would send me a person. God uses people as tour guides to help us transition into new levels. Many of my life milestones were marked by God sent connections who introduced me to the new level I had entered in my life. Some became best friends, and some were just seasonal. Regardless of our relationship now, I'm tremendously grateful for them.

Identify who God has strategically placed in your life and commit to better managing those relationships.

Unwanted Packages

Many people don't believe they need anyone. They wholeheartedly believe "they got it" all by themselves. This is another habit we need to exchange. We need people. There are people we are assigned to help, and there are people who are assigned to help us. The funny thing is, they don't always look like we expect them to. There are so many people who have something for us but look nothing like us. I call them "People packages." They're people who God assigned to deliver something at the doorsteps of our lives. Even though they aren't long term connections, God uses them to have a long-term impact on our lives.

One day, a custodian in my building gave me a nugget of wisdom that changed my perspective about work forever! Could there be someone who doesn't look like you, live where you live, or share your same interest who could be a major blessing to you? These could very well be your people packages. Don't miss them! God's plan for you far exceeds any cultural, racial or socioeconomic barrier there may be. See people past where they are and what they are doing. Be open to learning in strange classrooms. You never know what kind of package a true gift could come in! Unlike man, God looks at the heart of a person.

CHAPTER SEVEN

STRONG TIES, WEAK LINKS

God is fragrantly relational. He mightily moves through the avenue of relationSHIPS. Like any ship, relationships move. A God-ordained relationship will always do two things: take you somewhere good and produce something good. Get this, even if it does not always feel good! Through relationships, God allows you to go to new levels, achieve new things, and learn. When we experience toxic, mismanaged, or damaged relationships, it's tempting to shut ourselves off from meaningful relationships. Harboring on past hurt is one way the enemy tricks us into missing out on Godly connections. When two people get together, things begin to multiply and become stronger.

"1 can slay 1,000 and together two can slay 10,000." *(Deuteronomy 32:30)*

Notice that God didn't say together they slay 2,000 (as math would suggest) but rather 10,000! We must find the "together" of our lives. Who are you to be doing life with?

As I wrote this book, I prayed that God would guide my writing and put this book into the hands of the right people at the right time. My heart's desire was for this book to be a timely encouragement for all that read it. My downfall was that I was praying alone. Through the power of prayer, I alone was "Slaying 1,000" which is great. In my heart, I knew that this book was called to do more. I wanted it to touch more! I knew the power of books because books had led me on my path to living a sold-out life for Christ. Sure, I was saved, but I wasn't living for God. I went to church regularly, but I was just religious. I wasn't experiencing all that God offered me through a real relationship with Him. It wasn't at a church where I walked to the front and received true salvation. It was in my room. It was after reading this one little devotion for several weeks. What I read sparked an appetite for change in me. That little devotional stirred up my desire for Christ-centered living. Someone I didn't even know wrote a simple book that introduced me to God in a new way. I wanted that same blessing on my book. I wanted the book to travel to places that I didn't even know existed.

As I continued to write this book, a friend asked me if I had ever considered praying together for the success of my book. It was the answer to a thought in my heart. I wanted to slay 10 thousand, 50 thousand, or whatever God's will was for this book! So, I formed a prayer circle of seven people who prayed with me about the book for 21 days. I wrote out a prayer plan, and we prayed. We prayed for an anointing to multiply just like the scripture. Just like that, one of the biggest blessings in my life wasn't material, but a group of people who cared enough about me to pray intentionally for what God was doing through me. Of all that I owned, my relationships made me the richest.

In a world of *"I don't need anyone"*, *"I'd rather be alone"* and *"I've got this"*, we have to remember that we are truly better together. People are undoubtedly some of the greatest gifts God placed in our lives. It's not always what you have, but rather who you have that says a lot about how blessed you are. In addition to having the right people, we have to make sure we have them in the right place. Every opposite sex relationship is not a romantic relationship. Every friend is not meant to be our life-long *bestie*. Some relationships are seasonal, and some are life-long for good reasons!

Right Person, Wrong Place

Everyone isn't going to be like us, think like us, or look like us. People are different. We miss out on really great people because they don't fit the title we attempt to place on them. People are assigned to different roles in our lives and sometimes for different seasons. It is important to find out people's God-ordained position in our lives so we can experience strong and purposeful relationships. Those who are close to us, think similarly, share the same beliefs and values are strong links. They are consistent, and we value them the most. Others are temporary, think differently and distant in intimacy or closeness. Don't write these people off; they offer great value. Sometimes, those weak links can provide different perspectives. Everyone isn't a strong tie, and that's totally fine!

Friendships

In the world, people network and interact to further their career, influence, or agenda. While this is great, this is surface. There is more to connecting with others! Who are we actually making a connection with? Who are we choosing to walk through life with, keep us accountable and sharpen us when life seems to dull us out? Everyone won't be a friend, but someone is meant to be just that. It is difficult to go through life without a few people who can have access to the deeper parts of us.

Jesus had thousands of followers, twelve men He directly did ministry with, and three men who had intimate access to Him. If it was essential for Jesus, it is surely a model for us to do life successfully with others.

Friends will...

SHARPEN YOU They will inspire, motivate and even challenge you. It won't be comfortable, but these people are not here to keep you comfortable. They're here to help achieve the greatness God has for you!

VALUE YOU They will see in you what God sees in you. They won't degrade you, hold you to your past experiences, or not give you room to grow. No matter where you are in life, they will be able to see the good in you!

RESPECT YOU They will honor you and refuse to let you compromise your standards. They will have a high regard for you. What matters to you will matter to them.

CELEBRATE YOU They will be there for you when there's nothing to celebrate and applaud you when you've accomplished something great. They do not allow seeds of jealousy to take root and stop them from expressing their excitement for you.

Mentorship

One of the most underrated relationships is mentorship. Anybody doing anything needs a mentor. Mentorship is defined as personal development; a relationship in which a more experienced or more knowledgeable person helps to guide a less experienced or less knowledgeable person."

"*A less knowledgeable person*", it is this notion that keeps many people from investing into being mentored. Not many people want to admit that a little more knowledge could benefit them! But for anything we attempt to do, there's someone who knows something that could help us be better at what we do. Many of us perish not because of a lack of vision, courage, or drive, but a lack of knowledge! Without a mentor, we are at a disadvantage because we tend to spend more time figuring out things that have already been figured out. We continue to make the same mistakes over and over again because we don't allow ourselves to study and learn from those who are more proficient. Why are we willing to continuously make the same mistakes? Let's keep chipping at the iceberg together instead of trying to mold the same thing out of another block of ice! With a mentor, it could take six months to learn what may have taken someone else a few years.

Mentorship Myths

1. The mentor has to be older than the mentee.

Age does not always equal experience. A person can be 50 years old and know nothing about an area that a 30-year-old is very knowledgeable about. For example, a friend of mine is a 31-year-old financial advisor and may very well mentor an older person about investing, stocks and financial planning. In this case, age may be nothing but a number!

2. You have to be just like your mentor.

A mentor should be a person who helps shape and inspire the mentee to be who they are called to be. Mentors are inspiration, not the blueprint. As a mentee, your goal is not to become a cheaper version of your mentor. You should glean from the mentor to become the best version of yourself. Lastly, beware of hidden agendas! Be sure that the guidance from your mentor is genuine and not their way of living out their life's dreams through you.

3. A mentor can be anybody with expertise.

Although you don't have to be in the same state or city as your mentor, it is important that you have personal access to them. This may sound funny, but your mentor should know your name! There has to be a genuine, open, and honest relationship. It must be personal. Each encounter should be measurable by both the mentee and mentor.

The Recipe for a Good Mentee

HUMBLE A mentee cannot be prideful nor afraid to admit that they could use some help. Your mentor isn't successful because they knew everything. They are successful because somewhere down the road, they admitted that they needed help.

ABLE TO RECEIVE CONSTRUCTIVE CRITICISM As a mentee, you can't take things personally. After all, your mentor is there to help, right? You must embrace constructive criticism and be willing to be challenged. A mentee should not be looking for a "yes man" as a mentor. You need honesty and wisdom to be a better person.

The Recipe for a Good Mentor

MENTORS MUST NOT BE ENVIOUS A mentor cannot be jealous of the one they are mentoring. Period. The mentor should add measurable value to the life of the mentee.

UNSELFISH A good mentor should not be selfish with what they know. They must be open to sharing experiences wisdom and ideas. If this person is afraid of the mentee becoming more knowledgeable than them, they don't have the confidence necessary to be a mentor. A mentor must understand that sharing knowledge takes nothing away from them. It is only by the grace of God that we are where we are and know what we know.

MENTORS MUST NOT BE DREAM KILLERS The role of the mentor is to help the mentee acquire the knowledge, insight, and accountability necessary for them to reach new levels. It is not the role of a mentee to shoot down every idea, goal, or dream of the mentee. Prayer is essential in this relationship. A mentee must be wise about when to warn, and when to agree in faith.

MENTORS MUST BE A SOURCE OF WISE COUNSEL This is not the time to give personal opinions. Mentees need God-given wisdom. The mentor must be careful of sharing from a place of hurt or brokenness. One bad experience cannot be the source of the mentor's advice.

MENTORS MUST MOTIVATE This person should be uplifting and enlightening not a pessimist or an addition the mentee's problems!

Accountability Partners

An accountability partner is just that, someone you can count on. If they are someone who can not be counted on, revisit this person's role in your life. You need someone who will be available after hours to say a quick prayer with you or to remind you of the goals you are working towards. Your accountability partner should be someone you can share personal trials, shortcomings, and desires with so they can help you be accountable to the boundaries you have placed in your life. They should be a trusted person who is willing to tell you "no" when you need to hear it. Just like your mentor, your accountability partner can not be a "yes man".

Both of these relationships are essentials. They should add value to you and you to them. We need one of each so that we don't find ourselves doing life alone. See people as gifts to you and remember to be a gift to them!

CHAPTER EIGHT

THE METHOD OF MASTERY

Throughout our lives, we've experienced things we liked and things that we didn't like so much. We have activities we enjoy and activities we dread. When it comes to our purpose, we experience the same feelings. Even though we may love what we do, there are still certain aspects we could do without. As much as we want to do what we like and neglect what we dislike, it is important that we learn to love the entire process. To go from good to great, we must learn the method to mastery. We must master the things we are already good at and learn to love the part of the task that we don't necessarily like.

The key to mastery is staying motivated. When things are going great, it's easy to stay motivated. However, when times are trying, we find ourselves ready to throw in the towel. It would be amazing to have a personal cheer squad to root us on 24/7, but it's just not possible.

Friends, accountability partners, and mentors are great sources of motivation, but they are just that-- a source. It is not their responsibility to motivate you 24/7. After all, they have lives of their own. People will always be limited in their availability to you, and that's ok. You must learn how to motivate from within.

Self-motivation

If we don't know who we are and why we do, we're doomed to mediocrity at best. The reason many people cannot motivate themselves is because they have no clue who they are or why they do what they do. Self-motivation starts with self-realization. Realize more about who you are at your core. Ask yourself revealing questions like:

- Who am I?
- What are three areas of strength for me?
- What are three areas of weakness for me?
- What do I like?
- What do I not like?

Over the next few days, take notes on when you feel least motivated and when you feel like a superstar! Note little things such as:

- What time of day works best for you to interact with other people?
- What times are not good times for you to deal with others?
- Are you more of a morning or night person?
- When are you most inspired throughout the day?
- Are you more inspired with people or alone?
- Are there particular people who seem to bring you down?
- Are there people who inspire you more than others?

Most importantly, notice the difference in yourself on days when you don't spend time in the word of God and the days when you do. Chances are you don't have as much of a productive, motivating and peaceful day when you don't have that time with Him. If you don't spend daily time with God, I encourage you to do so. Start with a devotional and go back into your Bible to read the scriptures from that devotion. Select one of those scriptures to take with you throughout your day. Think about it. Say it over and over and allow God to speak to you about that scripture. Be intentional about hearing from God everyday. Don't just cram in time to say you read your word. Figure out when your time with God is most beneficial. Are you too busy during the day? Are you too tired at night? Pinpoint a time you are most in tune with God, make daily appointments, and keep them! These are just a few ways to jumpstart your self-realization.

Patterns

What are your patterns? After you take some time to realize who you are, you will recognize what works for you, and what doesn't. Once you are aware of these things, you will be able to work around and develop great daily motivators to implement into your lifestyle.

Hidden Agendas

Inside the word motivation is hidden the word "motive". Our motive is why we do what we do. When we identify the 'why' behind what we do, it can be used to motivate us along the journey of doing. When we hear people use the word 'motive' its most commonly used to suggest something bad or negative. For example, "I knew they had the wrong motive in raising the money" or "Her motives are never right." But 'motive' is a neutral word. There can be good motives, and there can be bad motives. We all have a motive behind why we do what we do.

For everything you do, define your motive. When you have the right motive, you are likely to stay motivated when living out your purpose gets hard. Your motive will determine whether you will stick in there when things get tough. It will determine whether or not you weather the storms and roadblocks along the journey of fulfilling your purpose.

Invest in Yourself

Things that are important are worth investing in! As a part of my profession as a Speech Language Pathologist, we are required to gather so many hours per year in continuing education. In other words, we are encouraged never to stop learning about the services we provide! If we are going to do anything, we should commit to growing in it. We should read as much as possible, attend conferences and other gatherings that will be beneficial to us growing in that area. As a believer, we should invest in ourselves spiritually. We should not be reluctant to purchase a great study Bible, journal and spiritual books. We should invest time into our relationship with God. To get much out of anything, we must invest time into it. If you plan to start a business, invest in conferences, seminars, and business material. If you can't seem to get things started or find yourself in a rut, invest in a life coach or someone who will offer resources and a high level of accountability. If you have a life crisis, need professional intervention, do not be afraid to do just that! Get counseling and coaching and choose to be the best you possible.

Check Your Pulse

It's important to check on yourself to see where you are. Whether or not you are accomplishing is extremely important. Even on your job, you're working for more than just what your boss tells you to do. You have an assignment. God uses so many things on our jobs and in our lives to mature us. We should always take self-inventory and evaluate our personal growth. When you take self-inventory, you ask yourself questions like, "Have I grown? Am I making progress? Am I sticking to my goals?

It's better to self-evaluate before you're evaluated by an external source. It's much less stressful and uncomfortable to correct ourselves before being corrected by someone else!

I remember being on a job during grad school. After working there for seven months, the manager suddenly sent out an email informing us that everyone would have to re-interview for the job we already had! I was shocked because I had never heard of such a thing. Thoughts raced through my mind. Had I been everything that I said I was during my first interview? Am I doing everything I need to do to secure my job? I immediately interviewed myself before re-interviewing with them. I had to be honest and admit that what I had mentioned as a weakness at the time of my first interview was still a weakness for me. I had not put any effort to progress in that area.

This is a problem of complacency! As soon as achieve our desires, it's tempting to get comfortable and relaxed instead of working hard to maintain what we have gained. We must be more concerned with living up to a new set of standards that don't change when we think no one is listening; We must have standards that create integrity and consistency.

God is always looking at our character. Our character speaks louder than our works or words!

Take time to answer the questions in this chapter. Grab a pen and pad and write your responses down. Paper exposes where we are. In addition to these questions, write down your schedule for your last three days.

Review how you spent the last 72 hours. A written schedule exposes what we do with our time. Be honest about where you are and make the necessary adjustments. You'll thank yourself later!

CHAPTER NINE

I'M FAILING AND I CAN'T GET UP

'm sure we can all agree that failure is uncomfortable. However, failure can be one of our best teachers. It all depends on our mindsets and perspectives. As for me, I will give a task all I've got before I fall face down in defeat. Once I get up, I'm able to pinpoint exactly where I fell short. This realization doesn't come from viewing everything I did right and questioning God about why I failed. This realization only comes when I review what I've done wrong. After I have a clear view of where I went wrong, I can try again without repeating the same unsuccessful methods. Failure is not the signal to quit, but rather, it reveals the recipe for future success! It's safe to say that many times, failure is only a speed bump along the road to success. We will fall, but unfortunately, many of us never get back up. We allow failure to slow us down to the point where we stop moving forward altogether. We were not created to be quitters. God designed us to be resilient. As resilient creations, we have the capable to turn setbacks into comebacks.

The Fear of the Crowd

The opinion of others has a way of stopping us dead in our tracks. When we fail, we concern ourselves with what others will say or think about us. Here's what we must understand: God didn't ask the crowd's opinion when He gave you your race to run! There comes a time when we must become free from the thoughts, opinions, and commentary of other people. So what if someone doesn't believe that you can get it done. It's not everyone's job to support you in accomplishing your personal goals. Our cannot always expect everyone to be there for us, but we can always count on God to be there. God is always for us. We must remind ourselves that God has the final say. We must constantly remind ourselves that God will use every hiccup in our history to create success in our future.

We are indeed victorious. God set things up so that we always win! Even winners have the option to quit. The difference between a winner and a loser is one who chose not to resign. Many winners tried quitting. If you've tried, trust me you aren't the first. Even Peter, one of Jesus' closest disciples, almost gave up on what He was called to do. One morning, Peter, a fisherman turned disciple, decided that he would go back to what he knew, fishing. Like Peter, a part of us desires to run back into the cushion of our comfort zone. Because we were designed to be winners, we must resist the temptation. As winners, we must allow God to stretch us and increase our capacity. We don't work in our own strength. We operate in the strength of God.

Reasons People Quit

1. They see failure as a sign to give up.
2. They fear the unknown.
3. They fear failure more than they desire success.
4. They resist change.
5. They live in their mistakes.
6. They have no vision.
7. They expect immediate results.
8. They have a lack of faith and a trust in fear.

Identify which one of these may be hindering you and then tackle it head on. Refuse to stay down. Never live where you landed after a fall. Move beyond your own sight and allow faith to be your new vision. Remember why you started and trust that God knows what you don't. The only way you can fail is by never trying in the first place. Keep going! Failure is only feedback that helps you grow!

CHAPTER TEN

DRIVING ON E

If you've ever almost ran out of gas, you are familiar with the rollercoaster of feelings that come along with riding on empty. It's no fun, pretty embarrassing, and can be quite frightening. Both you and the car become sluggish and unstable. Stress levels begin to rise and the anxiety of knowing that your car could stop at any moment can be quite overwhelming. You hope and pray that you'll make it to the gas station before you run out. In your mind, you think that if you can just get your car to the street in front of the station, you can roll in neutral over to the pump. You become certain that you have "just enough" gas to make it to the pump. I'm sure you laughed in agreement, just thinking of the many times you've done this. What's not so funny, is that so many of us live our lives this way. We operate on the edge with a "just enough" mentality. We have just enough money, just enough love, just enough joy, and just enough faith. We were not created to live on 'E'. We were created to live an abundant life. God is a God of abundance. His resources are undeniably limitless. The Bible assures us of that.

"The earth is mine and all that is in it."(Psalm 24:1)

In this scripture, God reminds us that He owns everything, and that there's nothing He does not have access to! He will make what He owns available for us to meet and exceed every need we have. Although God may use the resources of our jobs and people, He is ultimately our Source, the One who made the resources possible in the first place. The Bible goes on to say,

"And my God will supply all your needs according to His riches in glory in Christ Jesus." (Philippians 4:19)

God doesn't limit us to just the resources of the earth (our jobs, income and paychecks). He's willing to use the supply of Heaven (His riches in glory) to provide for us as well. He is able to do this for us. He desires to do this for us. With that in mind, why aren't our prayers bigger? Why aren't our request bolder? When is the last time you asked God for something impossible without Him? When is the last time you believed God for something bigger than yourself? Our prayers should consist of desires beyond our everyday needs. We should be praying for blessings big enough for ourselves and others!

Often, we are so concerned with what we need that we forget that God desires to do so much more. Think back on your life before you developed a personal relationship with God. Can you see how He met your needs without you even asking? He was our source before we knew Him as our source! God's plans are much bigger than having enough for ourselves. He needs us to share what He's given us with others. We were created to be an extension of God's hand to the earth.

We know we need to be a blessing to others. Many of us have a true desire to be a blessing to others. But, how can we be a blessing if we aren't blessed? We can't give money we don't have, we cannot share joy we don't posses, and we can't love if I don't understand the greatest love there is, Jesus. We must first have in order to give. It's great to give, but be mindful of what you are trying to pour out. If we are depleted emotionally, financially, spiritually and relationally, we surely can't help anyone else along their journey. No matter how much we try, it is impossible to pour from an empty cup.

Much like the gas gauge on the dashboard of a car, our lives can be compared to a meter ranging from empty to full. If empty is your norm, then you already know it's frustrating to never have enough. This is why we must allow God to continuously fill us over and over again. If He is not a regular part of our day, we will soon feel that same anxiety, frustration and freight of running out.

It's not about having *everything*. It's about having the faith to receive *anything you'd ever need*. Being at a place of empty is a faith matter, not a money matter. When we put some faith with the little we have, God is able to make our "little" more than we ever imagined.

When a *Little* turns into a *Lot*

In the Bible, we see clear evidence of Jesus' ability to create overflow where there was once lack. Remember the day Jesus fed over 5,000 men and women with two fish and five loaves of bread? Thousands had been listening to Jesus teach for days. They were so hungry that it would have been dangerous to travel back home on empty. One boy had a sack lunch prepared for him by his mother, so Jesus took the two small fish and five loaves of bread offered by the young boy. He used a lunch fit for a boy. That young boy's lunch was nowhere near enough to feed thousands, but He multiplied it and caused it to be sufficient. He used what "little" the boy had and made a miracle of it all because the boy was willing to give what he had. He can do the same for us! Even when we have nowhere near enough, trust God enough to return what He already provided. Watch Him do the miraculous with it!

God Must Like Leftovers

That same day, after 5,000 men plus the women and children had eaten the 'miracle meal', the disciples collected 12 baskets of leftover food. Twelve baskets full! Shortly after that miracle, Jesus does the same thing again. Later in his ministry, he fed another 4,000 with just a few fish and loaves. Yep, you guessed it, there were plenty of leftovers. God never provides without an abundance! He will give you enough for now and later. He gives enough for you and your neighbor. He's a God of more than enough!

So let's review the facts. Jesus came to give us an abundant life. He is the God of more than enough. He is able to exceed even our greatest expectations. All the earth belongs to Him. So, why have so many only experienced less than? It's simple. Satan has another agenda. He desires to steal, kill, and destroy all you possess. It's not because He cares about your stuff. He desires to leave you lifeless. If you aren't aware of the plan of our adversary, it's time you understood his scheme.

"The thief comes only to steal and kill and destroy; I came that they may have life, and have it abundantly." *(John 10:10)*

The enemy will do whatever it takes to rob us of our confidence in God's Holy Word. Do not allow the lies and deception of the enemy to steal your joy and your expectation in God. Guard your heart and your mind against the enemy so that he doesn't destroy your life! Maintain a strong relationship with God so that you are constantly filled with more of Him. Leave no room for the enemy in your life. Choose to live from the fullness of God and give from His overflow!

"My cup overflows. Surely your goodness and love will follow me all the days of my life,"(Psalm 23:5)

CHAPTER ELEVEN

THE CELEBRATION

We get so wrapped up in the day to day demands of life that we find ourselves moving from one task to the next with no break in sight. Seriously, when's the last time you celebrated yourself outside of your birthday, graduation, or anniversary? Celebration is important because it keeps momentum, motivates, and is incredibly meaningful. Much like a sports team, sometimes you have to celebrate between plays and not just at the end of the game! We must be deliberate in celebrating our life at every milestone. You can't treat everyday the same! Congratulate yourself for being consistent, remaining positive, and being available for God. That's truly something to celebrate. Personally, I rushed through many important milestones that I later needed as momentum to keep going. I learned that it's okay to celebrate the moments. In addition, we can't be afraid to celebrate others. Many times, we allow envy to set in because we refuse to be happy for those around us.

Small Victories

In order to stay motivated and have the courage to win the big battles of life, you need small victories in your back pocket! We are victorious people. Victorious people need to have victories! It's extremely motivating to have a record of what you've accomplished to remind you that you can accomplish again. We fear taking on the big tasks because we don't have any small wins to remind us that we are victorious. It's important that these wins be our own personal wins, not the wins of those around us.

In the Bible, David was a young guy who only had experience as a shepherd. He was courageous enough to take on a battle with Goliath, a seven-foot giant who tormented his people. For some reason, David was confident in going into a fight that others were not comfortable enough to go in. Maybe David hadn't defeated a giant before, but he had killed a lion and a bear! He was encouraged by reminding himself of what God had done for Him before. So he was sure that God would do it for him again just on a larger scale. In our own lives, it's one thing when God erases debt for someone else, but its another thing for Him to do it for you! It's one thing to hear of someone else's story but what about your own? Can you tell of any miracles God has done for you? Do you have memory of a personal miracle? There's something about reminding yourself of your story that builds your faith!

David was not accustomed to losing, so he went into the battle with an expectation to win! In the same way, our expectation should be high. Before we head into anything, we should remind ourselves of all the things God has already done! Expectation is an essential part of our faith. We have to keep expecting victory even when it seems impossible.

Surprise Parties

Surprise parties are neat. If done correctly, the person being surprised has no notion about the celebration. In this case, every celebration can't be a surprise party. If we are intentional in our prayers and specific about our requests, nothing should come as a surprise. Will we receive unexpected blessings? Absolutely, God is just that good! We can't, however, spend our lives *hoping* that God will do something good in our lives. When we pray, we must believe that it's just a matter of time before we see God's intervention. We should be intentional about being victorious. We will not stumble upon everything God has for us. We must pray boldly with great detail. When we witness a turn around in our situation, we know without a doubt that it was a move from God.

Private Parties

We work hard towards progress, so we must acknowledge when progress has been made. Every now and then, it's important that we celebrate those we love and believe in. Treat those who were a blessing to you to dinner, brunch, coffee, or dessert. This gives you a reason to celebrate them and forces everyone to pause and focus on the positive! Your ability to be happy for others determines if you can handle what they've achieved!

EnJOY!

The joy of the Lord is our strength. So enjoy yourself! Don't take yourself too seriously, and definitely don't rely on your own strength. Here's spoiler alert: We win! God fights all of our battles. Our only job is to trust Him. Don't find yourself worrying your life away. What can worry add to your life? Nothing! Choose to *enJOY*. Why? Because with God, we always win!

"But thanks be to God who causes me win!" (1 Corinthians 15:57)

CHAPTER TWELVE

I DO

"Today, I have given you the choice between life and death. oh, that you would choose life." (Deuteronomy 30:19)

At every wedding, the bride and groom make a binding commitment with these two words: "I do". My hope is that every reader either commits or re-commits themselves to their groom, Jesus Christ. I pray that you will become determined to live out the calling on your life, committed to doing whatever He leads and guides you to do, and determined to please Him without fear or reserve. With Him, all things are possible.

I,_____, commit and hereby accept the charge to exchange every distraction, be it past or present, to live life forward in purpose to please God. Wherever I go, I won't go alone. I will take Christ with me in my heart. I will find out why

He led me there and be obedient to whatever He tells me to do. May my life bring Him glory, forever.

Signature:_____ Date:_____

NOTES

I am proud of you. *Yes, you!* Committing to reading a book takes discipline and a strong will. Here's a big CONGRATULATIONS to you! Finishing this read may seem like a small (and hopefully enjoyable) goal, but it is still a goal nonetheless. Prayerfully, this book will be a tool to equip you with what you'll need to accomplish other goals and assignments in your life! Use the next few pages to write notes on what you have learned. Remember, the vision isn't real until it's on paper!

LAUREN A. WARD

LAUREN A. WARD

LAUREN A. WARD

LAUREN A. WARD

EXCHANGE

STAY CONNECTED

Thank you for purchasing Exchange! Lauren wants to hear from you! Stay connected by following Lauren Ward on Facebook, Instagram, and Periscope. For more information on booking, new releases, or other news from the author, visit: www.laurenaward.com.

FACEBOOK Lauren A. Ward

INSTAGRAM lauren_a_ward

PERISCOPE lauren_a_ward

Made in the USA
Charleston, SC
07 July 2016